For Chloe
who is the best writer I know and will publish her own
book someday soon.

Fundraising

How NAMIWalks
Can Change Your Community

By Blair Young

Library of Regress Cataloging-in-Publication Data

Young, Blair
        Fundraising – How NAMIWalks Can Change Your Community /
by Blair Young

p.em.
ISBN 978-1-257-11060-5 (alk.paper)
1. Conduct of Self – Wisdom, quotes, etc.
1. Title: Fundraising – How NAMIWalks Can Change Your Community.
11 Title
MHY56CHB84414
2010 838'TR.92-bdy,hey 566   2010577395

Blair Young books are available at special discounts when purchased in
bulk for premiums and sales promotions as well as for fundraising or
educational use or when ordered on days that end in the letter y. Special
editions or book excerpts can also be created to specification or not. For
details send your request on standard typing paper, double spaced and in
triplicate to the post office box address listed below.

This publication can also be purchased online at:
http://www.lulu.com/product/paperback/fundraising/12555170

Printed in the United States of America

First printing September, 2010
Second printing November, 2010
Third printing February, 2011
20 19 18 17 16 15 14 13 12

Table of Contents

The Best Way to Raise Awareness about Mental Illness
....Page 7

Ten Tips on Organizing Your NAMIWalk
....Page 11

The Joy of Fundraising
....Page 15

Nine Things that Everyone Should Know About Fundraising
....Page 21

Expand the Reach in Order to Grow Your Walk
....Page 25

Find New Sponsors When You Find New Friends
....Page 29

Invite Your Friends
....Page 33

NAMI Board of Directors Lead the Way in their NAMIWalks
....Page 35

Business Leaders are Supporting NAMI through the Walk
....Page 39

NAMIWALKS Supports Stronger Partnerships between Law Enforcement and NAMI Affiliates
....Page 43

NAMIWalks are Opening Doors to the Faith Community
....Page 47

Building Relationships Keeps Donors Coming Back
....Page 51

Key Connection Messages
....Page 57

NAMIWalk Online Fundraising
....Page 61

The Keys to Online Fundraising
....Page 65

Celebrating the Life of Michael Alexander Davis Johnson
....Page 71

Workplace Team Fundraising Challenge
....Page 75

The Best Way to Raise Awareness
About Mental Illness

One of the most powerful and effective ways to fight the stigma that surrounds serious mental illness and to educate the public about the prevalence, cause and treatment of the illness is telling your personal story of why you are involved in NAMI. Many of the misconceptions disappear when people talk about how a mental illness has affected themselves, their family and their friends.

Patrick Corrigan, Professor of Psychiatry at the Illinois Institute of Technology is the principal investigator at the Chicago Consortium for Stigma Research. Dr. Corrigan, a leading authority on stigma related to mental illness has stated in his findings that the most effective method to combat these erroneous beliefs is to expose people to an individual that is successfully coping with a serious mental illness, either directly or through their support system of family and friends. It is this personal contact, according to the Consortium's research, that allows the public to see mental illness for what it is – a disorder of the brain that strikes indiscriminately.

The foundation of the *NAMIWalks for the Mind of America* is the process that encourages NAMI members and supporters to write letters and send emails to everyone in their personal and professional networks to educate them on mental illness and NAMI. This personal communication is also the way to ask the reader to join and/or support the NAMIWalk in their community. It is through this letter and email campaign that we can begin to have a meaningful impact on the stigma associated to this issue and successfully reach out to the segment of the community that could benefit from knowing about NAMI programs.

Part of the problem mental health advocates face in the fight to eliminate the stigma is the stigma itself. It inhibits us from telling our stories in all but the safest environments even though we know that remaining silent allows many great opportunities to escape.

But because the NAMIWalk awareness and fundraising process provides some protection from the discomfort we might feel when talking about NAMI, we begin to lose some of the reticence we feel when sharing our personal stories. After all, everyone participates in walkathons and asking for this kind of support is a much more innocuous way of identifying ourselves as a mental health advocate.

Then an amazing thing happens – we find that our friends and acquaintances are anxious to be supportive and they respond in a much more positive and caring way than we expected!

The support of family and friends and the ever-increasing acceptance of mental illness as a treatable disorder make it easier to deal with the burden these illnesses impose on us and our loved ones.

Once we get comfortable, we begin to lose the self-inflicted inhibitions that the stigma creates which removes the hesitation we feel about exposing this information about ourselves. When that happens, we can begin to be the leader that we wish to be by being able to talk about mental illness and NAMI as naturally as we talk about any of the more accepted health issues all of our families face.

Through NAMIWalks, we are raising awareness and raising funds as well as developing the world-class advocates that we will need to remove the barriers that still exist as a result of the public's lack of understanding about mental illness.

That is why the emphasis is always on team building, walker recruitment and the email/letter writing campaigns instead of more superficial public education vehicles like billboard and media exposure. The Center for a New American Dream reports that Americans are now exposed to more than 1,500 commercial messages each day. It is unreasonable to expect that passing a billboard at 60 miles an hour or hearing a brief radio announcement about NAMI will be anywhere near as effective as a face-to-face interaction with someone that has a first hand understanding of mental illness. The research performed by Dr. Corrigan and others emphasizes that it is direct contact by peers whose families are impacted by this illness that forces the public to re-evaluate their perceptions about what mental illness is and who it affects.

The Walk model that has been developed by NAMI takes all these factors into consideration at every stage of the process from the selection of the walk location to use of the NAMIWalks website. We know that being seen by passing motorists as we walk does nothing to change their views of mental illness or NAMI. We also know we can change their views when we invite them to join us or support us as we walk because they are our neighbors, co-workers or friends.

Mental illness must stop being an issue that our communities are permitted to drive by. NAMI is dedicated to helping all communities begin using the NAMIWalk model to invite the kind of discussions that are needed to address the issues we feel are important.

Ten Tips on Organizing Your NAMIWalk

1) Work with your National Walk Manager to develop a written plan and then share it with the core group of leaders that you will be counting on to help you achieve your Walk's goals.

Run your Walk like a small business. Have a written plan that spells out all roles and responsibilities. Slot motivated individuals into those roles and equip them with everything they need to do a great job.

2) Use your website. Use it to communicate goals, thank your sponsors, highlight accomplishments, recognize successes, honor individual contributors, etc. Promote your web site on all your materials. This is your front door to the community so make sure it projects the image you want people to see.

3) Review previous records. See what's been successful before. Look for ways to improve upon the past. What worked last year that you want to build on this year? Who did a small thing in last year's Walk that might be counted on for more this year? What area did you try to get more participation from last year and needs more work this year?

Don't work in a vacuum. Your Walk should be a continuous process and you should be able to pick up from where you left off the year before if you want to keep growing. Build momentum and keep it going.
4) Set a specific timeline with completion dates for each stage of the process and then make that happen. Let

everyone know what needs to be done by what date and don't waiver. If you don't have an objective and don't share the importance of meeting that objective, it is very unlikely that you will end up where you need to be.

Make sure that your start date and end date for each stage of the Walk process are firm.

5) Actively recruit volunteers who can help you on specific tasks. Get more and better volunteers by going after them. Don't wait for them to come to you. Think about what skills you need in order to accomplish the goals and then go recruit the volunteers that fit those needs. Don't just accept any-willing-body and then have them attend meetings every month. Decide what needs done and find the right people to do it.

Advertise for specific help via newsletters and word of mouth. Be very strategic with this process.

6) Identify needs and define roles so that as you fill slots with volunteers you can always create the best match. Do it ahead of time and match your group's needs to each volunteer's skills and availability by including it in each position's description.

7) Use different people. Roll these positions over so you are bringing new perspectives and new networks into play. Double up, particularly for key positions.
Fill organizational roles well ahead of time with different people than on the last Walk, unless there is a good reason not to switch.

8) Start early to broaden participation. Expand the reach by making that your focus. Communicate to everyone involved that the goal is to grow the Walk and ask everyone how they think that can be achieved.

Put the word out early and often about what volunteers you need. Get plenty of them so no one feels overworked. Offer a volunteer sign-up sheet for different events at every meeting.

9) Have a plan to keep the leadership of your Walk connected to its progress and challenges. Use a strong communicator to help group and assign volunteers. Some people are a natural for this key role – find one and let them help you build a strong leadership team.

10) Set small group goals along the timeline and then monitor and share progress. Break the overall goal down into what's needed from each sub-group and involve everyone in the process of goal setting and communicate progress. That will reinforce the correlation between funds raised and their own efforts.

Summary
Your Walk's success depends on well you master several basic concepts. You need to plan your timeline; you need to communicate the strategies designed to meet your goals and you need to recruit the right people to get the job done. Focus on planning, communication and adequate (manpower) resources so you will be able to accomplish what you set out to accomplish and so your community will benefit from a successful Walk.

The Joy of Fundraising

Do you really want to keep raising money the same way you always have? Wouldn't you like to get off that treadmill of one-year-at-a-time grants, letters, and special events, with no assurance of sustained giving? This could be the year to break that cycle and build a new base of donors who understand and truly believe in your mission—donors who want to become involved in ways that are uniquely meaningful to them.

The NAMIWalks Program is built on an entirely new way of thinking about fundraising. So say goodbye to the old reality of scarcity and year-to-year survival and get ready to shift your thinking into the new reality of abundance and a system for building and cultivating lifelong donors.

The fundraising most of us know is based on a myth—the myth that there is not enough money to go around. Believing that myth creates a culture of scarcity in which nonprofit organizations feel they must compete with each other not just for funds and resources, but for their very survival.

We believe that this mindset is not necessary; in fact, it can even be an obstacle to achieving financial sustainability. The key to getting off the year-to-year fundraising treadmill and moving towards long-term sustainable funding is to shift your thinking and leave behind the myth of scarcity for a context of abundance.

Once you do that, you will see that resources can be abundant. Charitable giving in America has surpassed $250 billion per year in recent years, of which more than 80% comes from individuals, according to the annual report Giving USA. And, according to Claude Rosenberg of the New Tithing Group, Americans could substantially increase what they are currently giving to charity without changing their lifestyles.

Still, the myth of scarcity persists in shaping our thinking, our focus, and our actions. The NAMIWalks Model is based on a new reality, the reality of abundance. By following the model, you will find yourself operating from abundance and raising more money more easily than ever.

The Old Reality of Fundraising	The Joy of Fundraising
The myth of scarcity:	**The reality of abundance:**
• There is never enough money to go around.	• The resources you need are in abundant supply.
• You need to attract new donors each year to stay afloat and you need to find even more new donors to grow.	• Take better care of the donors you already have. They will attract others and become lifelong partners in your work.

The Old Reality of Fundraising

The Joy of Fundraising

The myth of scarcity:

The reality of abundance:

- In order to get people to give, you must entertain them and give them something first.

- Donors give to causes they truly believe in.

- Effective fundraisers convey the essence of their organization's work through well-documented and clearly-presented facts and statistics.

- While myth-busting facts are important, effective fundraisers know donors respond best when they are moved by powerful stories of how your work affects the lives of those you serve.

- All donors can be cultivated in the same way.

- Each donor is a special individual who flourishes when treated with a personal touch.

The Old Reality of Fundraising	The Joy of Fundraising
The myth of scarcity:	**The reality of abundance:**
• Volunteers give time, not money. Don't bother trying to turn them into donors.	• Volunteers and donors are motivated by the same reasons. Cultivate your volunteers with love and care and many will become lifelong donors.
• Everyone knows the traits and demographics of the ideal big donors.	• Today, anyone can become a major donor. Treat everyone who comes in contact with your organization as if they have that potential.
• Asking for money is a difficult and tricky business. And sometimes it is downright scary.	• Asking for money can be as easy and natural as picking ripened fruit—for both you and your donors.

The Old Reality of Fundraising   **The Joy of Fundraising**

The myth of scarcity:	**The reality of abundance:**
• Spend your time seeking out big, one-time gifts.	• Your most committed donors want to be part of your long-term growth and financial stability.
• Endowments are only for big organizations, not for smaller, lesser-known nonprofits.	• Every nonprofit, regardless of size, can have a fund that covers its annual operating costs.

* Modified from *The Joy of Fundraising,* Chapter One

Nine Things that Everyone
Should Know About Fundraising

Everyone understands the need for community fundraising but few people understand it. It can be fun or it can be scary. Your job is to take the mystery out of it and make it so easy to understand that people have fun and can't wait to get involved.

Myths about fund-raising:
- The process is a mystery
- You need a proven track record to be successful
- Corporations and foundations give most of the money

If the people you are relying on for your fundraising success think that what you are asking them to do is difficult and confusing, then you are not going to be successful. The walk manager's job is to take the mystery out of the process and make people comfortable doing what you need them to do. If they believe they cannot do the job, they will not. One of my favorite quotes is one by Henry Ford, American industrialist, founder of the Ford Motor Company who said, "Whether you think that you can, or that you can't, you are usually right." If your volunteers think the process is mysterious and impossible, you will find it very difficult to involve them in your success.

By the way, my other favorite Henry Ford quote is good to keep in mind when it seems everything is going wrong – "When everything seems to be going against you, remember that the airplane takes off against the wind, not with it."

The biggest single most common reason I hear from people for not helping is, "I have never done it before." Most of the time they don't actually say it, but that is what they are thinking. They don't help because they think they can't do it and they think they can't do it because they have never done it before.

How do you overcome that? Help them understand how to be successful! Lead them to success by teaching them how to be successful. Give them the tools and the encouragement that they need to get engaged and then support them as they begin to make a difference in your Walk.

It is your job to clearly describe the path to success. Don't allow people to harbor any misconceptions. If they believe that the secret is to write grants to foundations and corporations, then you will not get them to engage their friends and neighbors in a meaningful way. Don't assume that anyone know what you do. Tell them what you plan and tell them how the Walk will work for your community. Be clear and specific so that people will question and then drop their misconceptions.

Nine Things that Everyone Should Know About Fundraising

1. Organizations are not entitled to support; they must earn it.

2. Successful fund-raising is not magic; it is simply hard work on the part of people who are thoroughly prepared.

3. Fundraising is not raising money; it is raising friends.

4. You do not raise money by begging for it; you raise it by selling people on your organization.

5. People do not just reach for their checkbooks and give money to an organization; they have to be asked to give.

6. You don't wait for the "right" moment to ask; you ask now.

7. Successful walk mangers do not ask for money; they get others to ask for it.

8. You don't decide today to raise money and then ask for it tomorrow: it takes time, patience, and planning to raise money.

9. Prospects and donors are not cash crops waiting to be harvested; treat them as you would customers in a business.

This is not brain surgery. It is simply a case of developing a plan, communicating it clearly and then executing the plan in a timely manner. The process is a combination of common sense, hard work, preparation, courtesy, commitment, enthusiasm, understanding, and a belief in what you are asking others to support.

Expand the Reach in Order to
Grow Your Walk

In the retail business, it is a commonly understood principle that there are only two ways to grow your business – 1) find new customers, and 2) get them to come back more often and spend more each visit (help them be better customers.)

The same principle applies to growing your Walk. You need to find new sponsors and team captains while you help your current sponsors and team captains become more effective. This is a very simple concept but will be useful as you consider ways to expand your efforts. Let's talk about sponsors first

Finding more sponsors should be a year round focus of your effort. Who are they and how do we convince them that they should join us in the Walk? The reality is that we have relationships with hundreds of potential sponsors right now that are never even approached to join us in our efforts to promote a healthier community. If we stopped and inventoried every business connection we have professionally and personally and asked each of the members of our organization to do the same, the resulting list would provide us enough very good NAMIWalk sponsorship prospects to promote a significant growth each year. Every time we add a sponsor, we also add that sponsor's network to our un-worked prospect list. The fact that these lists are never compiled does not mean they do not exist. We cannot develop a strategy for expanding our reach and growing the Walk without the compiled and organized list of direct connections that we each posses in our own networks. This is an important step and is not as hard as it seems.

The reality is that this process gets easier as your Walk matures. As you bring sponsors in, you also build momentum and credibility for your event and you get connected to people (current sponsors) that can help introduce you to bigger and more lucrative sponsors.

Why would a sponsor help you find more sponsors? Put yourself in their shoes – they sponsor your Walk because they believe in what you are doing and believe that their relationship with you is positive. Right? So they would be the perfect people to convince others in their network to join them in supporting the NAMIWalks. The bigger the event becomes, the more each sponsor benefits. It is in their best interest to help you expand the list of businesses that become involved as sponsors. Open that door and you will immediately begin to experience the benefits.

You must stop thinking of sponsors as needing to be found one at a time. Think of sponsors as doors that need opened and once opened afford you a whole new area of opportunity. Remember – everyone is connected in the business community and once you have one part of that network in your hands, follow it so you become connected to the entire business community.

Sponsors support NAMIWalks not to help us. Sponsors support NAMIWalks to help themselves, their customers, their employees and their stockholders.

Keep this in mind and help your volunteers understand this as well so that they can approach their business contacts with that same attitude. If we understand the value we have for the business community, then why would we hesitate to invite them to join us?

We need more sponsors and we need more team captains to be successful and to grow our Walk. Look at this challenge by changing the way you look at the people involved in your Walk. Everyone has a network and everyone is connected to a significant number of different other networks. Understanding this is the first step toward helping people see themselves as a successful team captain.

The secret is coaching team captains on what it takes to be successful. The more successful teams you have, the more likely it is that the members of those teams will go on to be successful team captains themselves. Just as with sponsors, the retail growth examples works with team captains as well – find more and help the existing ones be better.

If you can establish that being on a successful team is a stepping stone to becoming a team captain, your Walk's growth become self-fulfilling. Who better to be next year's new team captains than last year's walkers? Consider all of your walkers as team captains in training and plan your growth around that model. Then when a walker becomes a team captain, they convert their past donors to walkers and we start the process over again with new walkers finding new donors while everyone involved builds bigger, better teams. This is how you begin to achieve the kind of exponential growth you need to fulfill your promises to the community. This is how you grow your walk.

Find New Sponsors
When You Find New Friends

Ann Moore, a member of the NAMI Vermont Board of Directors is one of the top team captains in the country. Ann told me recently that when she is asked how she does it, she tells people that raising money is the easiest things she does for NAMI because people appreciate what NAMI does and are always eager to be part of the Walk to show their support. She also advices anyone who will listen that the secret is to throw a wide net and that the more people you ask – the more people you will get to say yes.

Sponsorship campaigns work on the same principle. It is easy because NAMI does so much for the community that business leaders appreciate but have never been asked to support and the more you ask the bigger your Walk will be. The challenge is getting organized and helping the people involved in your Walk ask their friends to become our sponsors.

We can always use the Walk to make friends, but it is much easier to use the Walk to turn friends into sponsors. The better you are doing this, the bigger the Walk will be. Everyone involved in your Walk has dozens, if not hundreds of friends in the business world. Every single day each of us interacts with several potential NAMIWalk sponsors and many of them would be willing to support the Walk if asked.

So how do we have a significant impact on the rate of growth of our Walk's sponsorship campaign? I would say two ways and we have to use both strategies to be successful. First we need to redefine for everyone who we believe a good sponsor prospect is. Too many people you are talking to are thinking one thing while we are thinking something else. We need to be very specific and focus on this basic idea and be very clear when describing this expectation. When people hear 'Sponsor', they think $10,000 donor or they think about the companies in their community that are already connected to other local of regional events. In order to be successful in getting these people engaged we need to help them see that we are defining sponsor prospects as the business people they do business with everyday. We need to help them change their perceptions and accept the expectations we have established by giving them examples to follow.

This leads me to the second strategy, which is to use the leaders of your sponsorship campaign (who are also the leaders of your Walk) as examples for others to follow. This is very important because this is how many people will learn what we need and how it is done. Start with the walk manager and the NAMI staff and help them secure a sponsor or two and then share those stories with others so that everyone can see WHO we are approaching and HOW we turned our friends into sponsors. Then get the board of directors involved the same way. Find one or two that can lead the way and then make sure that everyone else sees exactly WHO they are asking and HOW they are turning their friends into sponsors.

The earlier you start the easier it will be to get EVERYONE in your organization involved. Once you have established a successful strategy and the momentum you need, use these leaders to inspire others within your Walk to do the same.

Earlier I mentioned two things I want to revisit. I said that you need to get organized and I stated that we can always use the walk to make friends. One of the biggest mistakes a Walk can make is to lose track of which businesses were asked to be a sponsor in the past and what they said when asked. It is very important to remember that we are using the Walk to develop lifelong relationships with the business people we invite to join us in out community walk for mental illness and that relationship does not start with the check and does not end after the Walk. It starts when we first tell them about NAMI's mission as we ask them to join us and it never, ever ends. If a business leader is asked to be a sponsor and declines, we should accept the challenge of developing a relationship with that individual so that they better understand the important work NAMI does on behalf of the entire community including their customers, employees and their employees' families. If we do this successfully – and make them our friend – then we will be able count on their support in the future.

Insist on keeping good records and help everyone involved in your sponsorship campaign understand that this is a year-round, never-ending process that can best be described as making friends and finding ways for our friends to get involved in our community walk for mental illness.

Invite Your Friends

One of the most powerful and effective ways to fight the stigma that surrounds serious mental illness and to educate the public about the prevalence, cause and treatment of the illness is telling your personal story of why you are involved in NAMI. Many of misconceptions disappear when people talk about how a mental illness has affected themselves, their family and their friends.

The foundation of the *NAMIWALKS for the Mind of America* is the process that encourages NAMI members and supporters to write letters and send emails to everyone in their personal and professional networks to educate them on mental illness and NAMI. This personal communication also is the way to ask that the reader to join and/or support the NAMIWALK in their community. It is through this letter and email campaign that we can begin to have a meaningful impact on the stigma related to this issue and successfully reach out to the segment of the community that could benefit from knowing about NAMI programs.

Every good fundraising letter or email should accomplish all goals of the Walk – raise awareness and funding for NAMI programs. These letters, written by walkers to their friends and colleagues, should each do their part to:
• To raise awareness about mental illness
• To increase community education and reach out to new families and individuals living with mental illness
• To support local NAMI affiliates

• To build a larger NAMI community

NAMI Board of Directors Lead the Way in their NAMIWalks

As the NAMIWalk program marks its eighth year in 2010, several significant trends are emerging. As more than 450 NAMI affiliates join the effort this year by participating and sharing the funds raised in the more than 80 Walks scheduled in 46 states, the most successful Walks share some common characteristics. Typically, the local leadership has a clear vision of how the Walk can be utilized to meet the objectives of their state organization and the local affiliates participating. This vision is communicated so that other individuals and organizations can enthusiastically join in order to be part of a successful awareness and fundraising effort in the community.

Successful NAMIWalks have one other common trait. They always have strong leadership that sets an example by taking ownership of the Walk and being leaders of the effort. When the NAMI Board of Directors supports their Walk – it can do well. But when the Board of Directors LEADS their Walk effort, it always results in a very successful process. If the leaders are committed and visible, the community will follow.

The Board of Directors of NAMI Austin led a very successful effort in 2009 and the community followed in one of the fastest growing NAMIWalks in the country. NAMI Austin's Board President Lisa Moore Yoch did what great leaders do – she demonstrated her passion and commitment for the Walk and then inspired others to follow. NAMI Austin's Board understands that they are the leaders of the NAMI movement in their community and that the Walk will only be as successful as they are committed to making it.

In 2009, the 13 members of the NAMI Austin Board of Directors each created teams and those 13 teams raised a total of $30,000 with Yoch's team (NAMI Fundraisin' Fools) of 38 walkers leading the effort. Yoch said that the Board discussed the need to take a leadership role and decided to establish aggressive goals for themselves. They then worked together and supported each other as they moved their 4th year Walk forward in a very big way last October. Yoch stated, "We knew that if we were to be successful that we were going to have to take a much more active role as leaders of our Walk. We all knew how important it was and decided to make a statement by stepping up and making it happen."

The Board is already fully engaged in planning another successful NAMIWalk in 2010. They will again be leading this effort as they walk at Auditorium Shores on October 2nd.

Last year was also a record-breaking year for the NAMIWalk in St. Louis. On May 30th 2009, NAMI St. Louis held the biggest, most successful Walk in the 6 years they have been in the program. As one of the original 11 NAMIWalks in 2003, they have managed to grow steadily over the years. Then in 2009, the NAMI St. Louis Board of Directors worked together with their staff to help their Walk take a big step forward. With 100% participation, the Board of Directors each formed Walk teams and raised a combined $27,000 while each member of the staff also formed their own teams and raised more than $16,000. NAMI St. Louis Executive Director Jackie Lukitsch said that the dedication of her Board made it easier for her staff and the community to get involved the way they did last year. "The Board really stepped up and took control of the Walk last year and are even more involved in our Walk this year," said Lukitsch.

NAMI St. Louis Board President Joe Yancey makes sure that the importance of a successful Walk is discussed at every Board meeting. "We feel that, as leaders we are most responsible for the success of our affiliate. We know that we need to raise awareness about the impact mental illness has on the community and we know we need to raise funds to provide our programs. It just makes sense to be fully engaged in something as important as the NAMIWalk program."

With another successful Walk in 2010, NAMI St. Louis feels they are making a real difference for the consumers and families they represent and the communities that support them. The Board has agreed that if they are going to have an impact and be successful, they must be the leaders that their community needs. And when the NAMI St. Louis Board of Directors lead – the St. Louis community follows.

Business Leaders are Supporting NAMI through the Walk

The NAMIWalk held last year in Minneapolis' Minnehaha Park was not just another walk. Along side the large turnout of NAMI family and consumer advocates, a team of more than 300 representatives from HealthPartners walked as part of their employer's commitment as a business sponsor of NAMI Minnesota's first NAMIWalk. HealthPartners, a large consumer-governed, nonprofit health care organization based in Bloomington, MN agreed to provide a leadership role, becoming a Presenting Sponsor and encouraging its employees to participate by creating teams online using the NAMIWalk website. That partnership produced an impact of nearly $50,000 that became a significant factor in the success of this first year Walk which went on to raise more than $232,000.

Sue Abderholden, NAMI Minnesota's Executive Director says, "The NAMIWalk program helped us build upon our relationship with HealthPartners, broadening it beyond senior executives to all of its employees. Now, as a result of our partnership other health care organizations and providers understand the need to come together to show support for people with mental illness and their families and to work together to improve access to and the quality of mental health care."

When Aileen Brady, the NAMI Nebraska Walk Manager began discussing the possibility of participating as a NAMIWalk sponsor with Craig Wolf she had no idea how successful the relationship would become. Wolf, the Vice President and General Manager of Aureus Medical Group, a division of C&A Industries which is a national leader in the staffing industry and based in Omaha agreed to become a business sponsor of the Walk. As a past supporter of NAMI, Wolf agreed to become the Business Team Chair of Omaha's first Walk held in June. C&A Industries made a significant financial commitment in support of the Walk and agreed to host a NAMIWalk information meeting for its employees so they could learn how to get involved. Through this effort, and under Craig Wolf's leadership, C&A Industries created a team of nearly 300 walkers and raised nearly $30,000 in addition to their employer's sponsorship commitment of $10,000.

While the 2008 NAMIWalk in Omaha was a huge success, Brady is already working on recruiting the 2009 Business Team Chair with Wolf's connections in the Omaha business community. C&A Industries will return as a 2009 sponsor and will have a walk team as well, but Brady and Wolf understand the need to help other large local companies get connected to NAMI through the walk program.

NAMIWalks for the Mind of America, the largest mental health awareness program in the country is also one of the fastest growing walk programs. NAMI's signature public education and fund raising event will be held in more than 70 locations and will raise more than $7.5 million in 2008 involving more than 100,000 walkers and supporters.

As NAMI affiliates and state organizations have quickly discovered, the NAMIWalk program is providing tremendous opportunities to get connected to the business community. As these business connections are being developed and nurtured, leaders in the business community are learning about NAMI and how to work together to improve the health of the community. Employers and retailers understand how dependent their success is on their communities' health and have begun to see NAMI as a valuable resource.

As more and more NAMIWalk programs develop relationships with their local business communities, several significant goals of the program begin to be realized. The Walk program is allowing advocates to educate corporate leaders on the facts of mental illness and to show them how active and strong an organization NAMI has become. Raising the public's awareness of mental illness is a much easier task if we have the business community assisting us.

Nothing is more powerful than seeing a NAMIWalk event with a list of sponsors that includes banks, manufacturers, retailers, insurance companies and employers of every type. Developing broad community support for the Walk means we are working together on an issue that affects us all. This very powerful message is one that is not lost on the general public. When they see a wide array of support from across the entire spectrum of the local business community, it reinforces this message.

Beginning in 2005 when David Underriner, the CEO of Providence Healthcare agreed to be the Business Team Chair for the NAMI Northwest Walk in Portland, OR the corporate community has agreed to work with NAMIs everywhere to build healthier communities.

Mary Brainerd, NAMI Minnesota's Business Team Chair and President/CEO of HealthPartners says, "The work we're doing with The National Alliance on Mental Illness (NAMI) is important because I firmly believe that the root of the problem begins and ends with the stigma against mental illness."

NAMIWALKS Supports Stronger Partnerships between Law Enforcement and NAMI Affiliates

Across the country, state and local NAMI affiliates are becoming more active and visible partners in their communities as a result of their participation in the *NAMIWALKS for the Mind of America* awareness and fundraising program. More than 100,000 walkers will participate in 78 Walks in 46 states during 2010 raising an estimated $8 million for NAMI programs in their affiliate areas.

The nationally recognized Crisis Intervention Team (CIT) law enforcement training is one of the programs that a growing number of NAMI affiliates are supporting with their funds. Designed to assist communities to better react to the problems created when law enforcement is called to respond to an individual in a mental health crisis, CIT is a community collaboration that requires treatment providers, criminal justice and consumer/family advocates to work together.

Although there is a significant training component to CIT, the most important and durable results of a successfully implemented CIT program are the relationships created between and among all local partners.

In communities as diverse as Houston, Texas; Chicago, Illinois; and Lake Charles, Louisiana NAMI affiliates are working closely with their local law enforcement leaders to better serve individuals with a serious mental illness and their families.

Lt. David Anders is the CIT Coordinator for the Lake Charles Police Department program, started two years ago with the help of NAMI Southwest Louisiana. Lt. Anders flatly states, "Clarice (Raichel, Executive Director of the NAMI Southwest Louisiana affiliate) was the driving force behind getting CIT kicked off in Lake Charles."

Among the many benefits that have been derived from implementing CIT in Lake Charles, Lt Anders cites the close working relationships that have developed between local law enforcement and the mental health treatment community. "I can pick up the phone to call the director of the inpatient unit at the psychiatric hospital anytime I need assistance because I was given his cell phone number. That would not have happened two years ago."

Lt. Anders is quick to point out that the network created when their CIT program was started has yielded significant benefits for his department, saying the "barriers and walls have come down and new doors have been opened."

As a result of this relationship, the Lake Charles Police Department and other law enforcement agencies in the surrounding areas have become big NAMI supporters and are very active in the *NAMIWALK* hosted by NAMI Southwest Louisiana. Last year, the department support staff held cake and cookie sales in the office to raise money for their team in the Walk. On Walk day, the Lake Charles Chief of Police was part of the 25 officers that participated in addition to more than 45 members of the Sherriff's Department and the Ward 3 Marshal's Office.

NAMI Greater Chicago has taken a leadership role and was instrumental in the development of the CIT program at the Chicago Police Department. CIT Officer Carrie vonSagun organized a team of police officers named "The Blue Minds" for the *NAMIWALK* in Chicago. Officer vonSagun said that getting the word out about their CIT program was a driving force behind the idea of walking with NAMI. "I believe it is very important that people know about NAMI and understand how CIT is changing the way the police are serving the community. We wanted to support NAMI and help educate the community on the ways we are working together."

In one of the largest CIT programs in the country, Lt. Mike Lee of the Houston Police Department organized a walk team of 50 officers and their families in support of the NAMIWalk in Houston. Lt. Lee said his officers were eager to participate. "We have a great relationship with NAMI and we walked because we wanted to show our commitment to what they do for the community."

Lee plans to have a much larger team of officers in next year's NAMIWalk with representatives from all the area law enforcement agencies participating in the CIT program. "We feel our participation in the Walk demonstrates to the public that we really do care. The officers that walked enjoyed the chance to get to know NAMI better and said they saw the impact the Walk can have on a community."

NAMIWalks are Opening Doors
to the Faith Community

Individuals living with a serious mental illness and their families have long depended on NAMI's education and support programs for the strength needed to cope successfully with the myriad of problems associated with these illnesses. From the moment of discovery that there is a support system to rely upon and the realization that we are not alone in this journey, NAMI members add their strength to a local network that in turn can more easily help others yet to need it. As NAMI's influence within its community grows, so does its capacity to serve a larger, broader base of its citizenry.

Like many Americans, the support and comfort that we find as active members of our faith community are important parts of our daily lives. We have learned to rely upon the wisdom of the leaders of our faith community to help us deal with everyday challenges as well as larger questions. The important part that faith plays in our lives is often dependent on the comfort and safety that belonging to a church, synagogue or mosque provides. That comfort and safety is never more important that when we face issues that challenge our well being or that of our family.

The leaders of our faith community are called upon to serve in an increasingly challenging society and are asked to provide guidance and comfort on an ever widening array of issues. The counsel offered by those leaders is an essential part of how we cope with the unexpected twists and turns that our lives take. It should not be a surprise to find that one of the issues our faith community leaders are called upon to address is that of undiagnosed mental illnesses in many of the families that they serve.

Several years ago, a prominent local pastor described the problem that is created when a faith community leader is not educated about mental illness and is not prepared to offer support or guidance to a member of the congregation asking for help. He said that bringing your mental illness into your faith community can become a 'two skunk problem.' He told a story about a woman that called the animal control office and reported that she had a skunk in the basement. The advice she got was to open the basement doors and drop a line of breadcrumbs into the woods. The next day when she called back, the animal control office asked if that worked, to which the woman replied, "Now I have two skunks in the basement."

If NAMI isn't connected to the faith community and offering support and education to its leaders, it is likely that they will not be able to effectively counsel those members that most need it. If a mother asks her pastor for understanding as she copes with a child that has been diagnosed with a mental illness, the pastor may not be able to provide the appropriate help and support. And, worse - may do nothing to help other parishioners understand and be supportive. For that mother, the result is that her last reliable support network – her faith community – is now lost to her as a result of sharing this issue. The challenge of living with a mental illness in her family and her decision to share it with her pastor created a second problem – the loss of the sanctuary of her faith community.

NAMIWalks, NAMI's signature awareness and fundraising program is growing and expanding to new communities every year. Since 2003, more than $45 million has been raised in more than 350 Walks with nearly one million walkers and donors. State organizations and NAMI affiliates are using the opportunity afforded by the Walk to reach out to the leaders of their local faith community to develop relationships that benefit everyone that relies upon those support systems. The results many Walks are reporting include opportunities for NAMI to provided printed materials or make presentations to lay leaders in the congregations that become involved in the Walk. By walking together, the community is better served and mental illness is better understood. By working together, we become familiar and more easily reliant on each other.

By utilizing the Walk to introduce NAMI and our message of hope, we open the door to an important partnership that will grow to strengthen the population we all serve.

Building Relationships
Keeps Donors Coming Back

According to Merriam-Webster, "credibility" is the quality or power of inspiring belief. The next part is to ask what inspires belief more than anything else. The answer is trust.

Trust is built from shared experiences and honest conversations, in good and bad times. It is fostered by doing what you say you'll do, when you say you'll do it. Trust is strengthened by coming to the aid of others when needed. But, what does trust have to do with building relationships with donors?

Everything.

Trust is personal. It's a value shared between individuals. Why does the long-time friend of your new executive director, now donate to your organization? Is it because he likes your mission? Maybe, but initially it's because he trusts and supports his friend.

For thousands of nonprofits, it's these types of personal and professional relationships that will be the saving grace in what will continue to be a year of uncertainty.

We tend to get caught up in trying to implement the next new whiz-bang, quick-win fundraising tactic. When we focus on that alone, we neglect old-fashioned relationship-building with those in our community. It's imperative to take the time to get out from behind our computer and in front of business owners, service groups, and like-minded individuals who might be able to help keep our organizations strong, and our missions moving forward.

Yes, word of mouth is still important. Word of mouth is a powerful marketing tool, and it's at the very core of viral marketing. It can be a powerful fundraising strategy for nonprofits. NAMIWalks is nothing if not a massive word of mouth generator because it encourages individuals within our organization to talk to their friends about what NAMI does in the community.

Using word of mouth to build relationships and influence for your organization can create a positive buzz within the community; increase contributions from current donors, while improving donor retention; and bring new donors to the organization. In fact, the *Great American Donor Survey*, conducted by Campbell Rinker, found that 85 percent of donors say they frequently or occasionally recommend one of their favorite charities to a friend or family member.

Encourage your board, volunteers, and staff to take advantage of opportunities to talk about why they're passionate about your organization in everyday business and personal interactions. Even casual conversations plant seeds in the minds of others that can be cultivated over time, as well as reinforced by other communications. Emphasize the opportunities created by your NAMIWalk to make these connections and then support the process of maintaining and strengthening the connections.

Your organization will be introduced to more people in a more positive light than through traditional marketing or public relations alone. When you finally make that ask for support, those people will be more inclined to give, because you have the support of their trusted friends and colleagues.

Local service organizations, such as Rotary, Kiwanis, and Lions clubs, are a great way to initiate these relationships. These organizations mobilize thousands of individuals whose time and contributions impact local, national, and international initiatives, such as hunger prevention, literacy, and medical aid. Shouldn't they also be given information about NAMI and have an opportunity to get involved through the Walk?

Service organizations enjoy learning about new groups and new projects, particularly ones in their local community that align to their strategic initiatives. Try to secure speaking opportunities at local service organization meetings to introduce your organization; educate them on the current trends or conditions that make your cause invaluable to the community; and, over time, gain new supporters.

Businesses provide much-needed resources to the nonprofit sector in terms of volunteers, monetary support, pro-bono services, and in-kind donations. Business networking organizations, such as Business Networking International (BNI) or your local Chamber of Commerce, can help you tap into your area's local businesses, resulting in increased awareness for your cause, and the development of key relationships with local business influencers in your community.

It's essential to developing a true partnership that helps both the business and your organization. When approaching possible new business partners, find out what they need to do to "move the needle" and foster inter-organizational trust by developing a two-way street for communication. Demonstrate how their involvement in your organization will help them accomplish one of their goals, like reaching new customers.

Once the trusting relationship is built, the businesses will naturally become advocates of your cause, spreading the word to their customers, clients, and business associates on your behalf. Getting your Walk sponsors actively involved in the Walk by attending the Team Captain Kick off Luncheon and Walk Day itself will connect them more securely to your organization and will be a long term advantage long after the money they donated was spent.

Making time is important. Even if you can only start small, start somewhere. We're all being asked to do more with less, and it's your relationships with supporters that will get you through these challenging times. Schedule time -- even just 15 minutes each day -- to focus on mobilizing your most devoted supporters to be advocates for your organization.

Strong organizations have pillars of strength around them. Fostering trust between your organization and its stakeholders in the community is a strategic activity that will pay for the investment in the long run.

The more people who speak highly of your organization, the greater the chance that your current and potential donors will hear messages of credibility and value in casual conversation, thus contributing to your cause.

Key Connection Messages

The success of the NAMIWalk will depend in a large part on how well the Walk Committee does in building a core of support among advocates and your partners in the behavioral healthcare system in the immediate area of your Walk. One of the long term objectives of the Walk is to have a positive impact on the public's perception of mental illness and raise awareness of NAMI and the programs that NAMI offers. This can best be done by using the Walk model to reach first into the networks of our natural allies (behavioral healthcare treatment providers) and then through them to the entire community. But we have to build the base of the Walk and make it as strong as possible by creating partnerships with these natural allies.

One way to do that is to consistently talk about shared organizational goals.

- NAMI is committed to educating the public in order to reduce and eliminate the stigma that inhibits access and adherence to treatment opportunities. The behavioral healthcare treatment community should share that goal.

- NAMI has been a passionate advocate in support of a fully funded system of behavioral healthcare treatment services. NAMI understands that we need educated and supportive elected officials and policy directors, which is much easier to achieve when there is a growing consensus in the media, in the business community and among the general public for the need for these services.

The behavioral healthcare treatment community should share that goal.

- NAMI provides family support and education, which increases the likelihood that our loved ones will remain in treatment and improves the chances that treatment providers will be successful in helping consumers maintain their recovery. The treatment providers need a strong NAMI.

- The primary healthcare system is serving consumers that NAMI represents in numbers far too great as individuals with a serious mental illness present themselves in emergency rooms demanding high cost (and uncompensated) care for untreated symptoms of their illness. The primary healthcare system would benefit greatly from partnering with a strong, supportive NAMI.

Our challenge is to deliver this shared vision with our natural partners and help them see that their mission would be well served by joining NAMI in our efforts to educate the public through our NAMIWalks. We are not asking for help - we are offering it.

We should do everything we can do to institutionalize this message AND get the full buy-in from NAMI advocates on the ground in the immediate area where the Walk is planned. Our chances of receiving full support from these natural partners increases tremendously when we are working closely with the consumer and family advocates that are most directly dependent on this system of care.

The next step is to expand our reach beyond the healthcare system. We must begin efforts to reach deeply into every part of the business community, meaning employers and retailers. The business community does not need a lesson from us on the importance of maintaining a healthy community. After all, they hire staff and attract customers from the public that we serve. We are important to them. What we do has great value to them. What we need to do is to be more visible to them and the Walk is the perfect way to begin that process. Everyone connected to the Walk (local affiliates and their members/supporters) should be coached and encouraged to understand the opportunity that exists and support them in their efforts to reach this segment of THEIR community. The better job we do of making this connection for them - the better they will do in connecting to the businesses in their community.

Your Regional Walk Manager is committed to working with you and helping you build this base for 2008 and beyond. Please begin this discussion at the Walk Committee level and get your Regional Walk Manager to assist you in this effort. We are determined to be the best resource possible to you and your volunteer committee.

60

NAMIWalk Online Fundraising

Sarah Sheahan

When I first started as NAMI New York City Metro Walk Manager, I could not imagine why anyone wouldn't register and fundraise online. Over the years, I have received emails from friends, family and acquaintances asking for a donation to support whatever walk, run, or other fundraising activity they do. I have always found online donations to be an easy way to support these community events.

After our first walk meeting, I realized that not everyone was comfortable with online fundraising, so I invited people to call me for help. The day after the information meeting I started getting calls. People did want to sign up, but they wanted help. So I helped because I knew the time I spent now would pay off later.

By the kick-off luncheon, I had a few walkers signed up, but the best part was that I had people in the audience that I had coached through the process during a phone call who could give testimony that it was easy to do and that I was willing to help them.

The thing to remember is that people are afraid of the technology AND they are afraid to ask for money. But more importantly, they DO want to be part of the community which is something that they are able to do when they have a walk page.

One of the dynamics of the NAMIWalks walker page is that allows donors to be part of the competition we create. Walkers without a personal page don't raise nearly as much as walkers with a personal page. In my Walk, walkers without a personal page only raise about 15% of what walkers with a personal page raise. One reason is that I remind walkers to donate to themselves first. This is crucial to building up online donations. You can have lots of walkers signed up, but if they do not donate to themselves, they are less likely to raise as much money.

Another factor in this is that nearly all online donations on a walker's page are the exact same amount. Part of having a walker page is that donors can see what others have given and are likely to give the same amount of money as previous donors.

That first donation sets the expectation for all donations to follow. It also shows the potential donor that the walker is committed to what is being asked of the donor and in turn makes them more committed towards the walker.
A benefit of raising money online is that it is an immediate donation - people don't hold off on a letter, they can click right through so it is easy for donors.

People do not like to ask for money and people do not know who to ask. The online walk page eliminates these two barriers which help raise funds.

Another benefit is the convenience of online giving. If they were to ask a friend in person, they probably would like to help, but don't have their checkbook or much in cash. Asking online makes this much easier.

So when talking about online fundraising, talk about how easy it is to ask for money using the website and emails and that it is easy to connect to a much bigger circle of friends through email and the web than you can face to face.

The Keys to Online Fundraising

First of all, like the Walk itself – the primary benefit of using the full potential of the NAMIWalk website is the opportunity to more effectively raise awareness about mental illness and how affects the entire community and specifically how we are involved. Using the NAMIWalk website to connect people to this issue and the hope that NAMI offers is one of the best and easiest ways to educate the public on this important issue.

If we develop and implement a comprehensive plan to get as many teams and walkers registered with personal web pages and inspire them to take full advantage of this tremendous tool, one of the outcomes is that many more people in our community will be aware of the issue and how it impacts families just like their own.

So the challenge is to motivate and inspire your network to embrace this goal and help them see how to take full advantage of the opportunity that the Walk model presents to spread the word in order to change people's perceptions of mental illness and recovery.

Here are several topics around which you can develop your presentation:

- Team Captain Outreach
    - Establish expectations early by institutionalizing your messages about what a team captain does by listing their responsibilities and helping them follow

the model. Team Captains' main responsibilities are:

- To recruit walkers for his or her team
- To see that those walkers are properly registered for the Walk
- To help those walkers create personal web pages and show them how to effectively use this tool
- To teach and encourage those walkers to gather as many donations as possible in support of their participation in the Walk
- To lead by their personal example in gathering donations for the Walk
- To communicate regularly with the NAMI volunteer(s) or staff person in charge of the Walk
- To communicate regularly with the walkers on their team about the Walk
- To make sure that the team has a team identity the day of the Walk (by having things like team T-shirts, team hats, team signs or banners or anything else that they can think of that will make the walkers on their team feel and look like a team at the Walk)

- Team Captain Coaching

- o Assume that all team captains will benefit from assistance in implementing the details of their responsibilities and offer suggestions and advice on how to be a successful team captain and how to develop a successful team
  - o Be economical with email blasts to team captains by repeating their core responsibilities and offering suggestions on how to accomplish the tasks
  - o Enlist the assistance of volunteer(s) to provide individual coaching to team captains as a way to solve problems that you were not aware of and to help more team captains achieve success
- Team Captain Communication
  - o Develop a plan for regular email communications with your team captains in order to provide reminders of their promise to recruit walkers, raise awareness and funding for NAMI programs AND with the useful information that will make it easy for them to follow the plan
- Sample letters and emails for awareness and fundraising
  - o Begin by sharing any and all past letter and email samples and ask all team captains to share their own personal letters with their walkers and copy the Walk Manager
  - o Encourage walkers to share their letters with others on their team along with a

brief word about the results of their letter campaign. Sharing letters is good, but including the results is event better – both dollars raised and the positive encouraging comments received as a result

- Team Goals
  - Help team captains arrive at a meaningful but challenging team goal based on the team's achievements the previous year and the potential of the collective members of the team this year. Suggest that they break the goal down to include online fundraising and communicate this goal with the members of the team
  - Encourage team captains to reference the team's progress toward their goal in all communications with the members of their team and to acknowledge milestones as they are passed along the way to meeting and exceeding their team goal
- Fundraising and Team Building incentive drawings
  - Develop an incentive program that will serve to reinforce the activities upon which you have built your online fundraising campaign. Solicit gift certificates and other prizes that can be used to motivate and reward all team captains to follow the steps necessary to be successful. This weekly drawing can

be established for team captains that qualify in categories such as:

- All teams that get two more walkers registered online this week
- All teams that have more than 75% of their walkers with personal web pages
- All teams with at least half of their walkers raising online funds
- Al teams with the majority of their walkers listing their own personal donation as the first donation on their personal page
- All teams that have met or passed their goal for walkers recruited
- All teams that have met or exceeded 25% of their team fundraising goal (or 50% or 75% or 100%)

- The benefits of emphasizing online fundraising
  - Easy for walkers to solicit more people easier
  - A way for walkers to ask friends and family for donations without needing to do it face-to-face or on the phone thus reducing their discomfort with the process
  - Easy way for donors to respond to a request since they can do it from their computer with their credit card instead of being asked to have a check or cash on hand for a face-to-face ask

- o Increases the average donation size since donors are able to use credit card
- o Multiplies the number of people that each walker can ask since email allows them to include friends and family in other parts of the country
- o Easy for Walk Manager because it reduces the amount of checks and cash turned in and all of the record keeping that requires.

Celebrating the
Life of Michael Alexander Davis Johnson

"Michael loved his family and friends – I know this as deeply as I knew Michael. And he knew we loved him and that was important to him. That mutual love is what we hold onto today, as we sort through the pain of this loss. What we are left with today are our memories."

These are the words that Janet Davis, Michael's mother shared with family and friends at the memorial service after Michael's life was lost to mental illness on March 21st, 2008 at the age of 21.

Michael was a student at Glendale Community College near Los Angeles with dreams of living in New York City and playing in the NBA, being an artist, a musician or a chef – all dreams built on areas of his life where he had shown talent. As a child he had overcome many obstacles – stuttering, reading problems and other language-related disabilities.

But in spite of the best medical care he was receiving, the symptoms of schizophrenia had hit hard. To his mother it seemed the Michael she knew begin to disappear. The voices became stronger and more violent.

At the time of Michael's death, Davis was attending NAMI's Family-to-Family classes. "NAMI was very helpful. Family-to-Family helped me understand Michael. It helped me understand why he did some of the things he did," says Davis.

Wayne Baldaro, the Walk Manager for the Los Angeles NAMIWalk said he first met Janet when she came into a support group he was running. "She was very open about her son. She wanted to connect with people with similar situations and experiences and wanted to learn about her son's illness," says Baldaro.

Davis told family and friends that she didn't want flowers and that she had just heard about the awareness raising and fundraising walk that NAMI does. She let people know that she prefer donations go to NAMI.

After Michael's death, Baldaro was asked to help Davis create a memorial page on the Los Angeles NAMIWalk website. Davis says, "I liked the NAMIWalks website because it gave me a chance to create something in Michael's memory that people could see. It was really easy and I liked having a picture of Michael with his brother as part of that."

More than 250 people attended Michael's memorial service. The printed program included information about NAMIWalks with the link to the web page that Davis created. "I was amazed at how many friends contributed. We would rather help others by doing this. It gave me comfort to read the comments left by our friends. The NAMIWalks web page allowed me to create a visual supportive community."

"If you start counting the number of people that have been deeply affected by Michael's death in his immediate family you realize what an impact this illness has," says Davis.

Davis remembers the problems that she encountered trying to get Michael into the treatment programs that he needed. "When you are in the middle of it you don't realize how awful it is." Davis, a professional development advisor for the public school system would like to write a book about the problems a mother faces trying to get help for her son. She would like to do whatever she can to help others understand the illness and problems her family dealt with even though Michael was in treatment and trying to recover from his illness.

"I encourage everyone to be open about the illness and the issue. It is shocking and surprising the number of people who have relatives with a serious mental illness. Two of my co-workers had children who were lost to mental illness," say Davis.

Davis is thankful for the opportunity that NAMIWalks has given her to celebrate Michael's life. "I have a discomfort asking people for money, but I realize that if you give people an opportunity to help – they will. It makes me feel good that we did something good – that I did something positive."

Davis looks forward to participating with her family and friends in the Los Angeles Walk in Santa Monica. She believes it will be a wonderful way to remember Michael and be thankful for the chance to make more people aware of how mental illness affects families everywhere.

At the suggestion of her future daughter-in-law, Davis includes the following line at the bottom of all of her emails:

To help advance research on schizophrenia and to support those who are touched by this devastating illness, please make a donation in memory of Michael Alexander Davis Johnson, to: http://www.nami.org/namiwalks08/LOS/formichael

Davis is determined that something good will be created out of the terrible tragedy she has endured and is thankful to NAMI for that opportunity

Workplace Team Fundraising Challenge

The best way to raise awareness and funds for mental health education programs is by asking friends, family and neighbors to go to your personal web page on the NAMIWalk website and make a contribution in support of your participation in the Walk. The more people we touch with this process, the fewer people there are in the community who do not know that recovery is possible if treatment is available.

An excellent way to encourage Walkers on a workplace team to conduct vigorous email campaigns using the NAMIWalks website is to create challenges between teams and to create team activities designed to raise additional funds but also designed to get more people in the workplace to participate because of the fun everyone is having. Here are several ideas that have worked in other Walks. I am sure one of these (or a variation) can work for you.

Workplace Fundraising Tips for NAMIWalks

- Consider recruiting a team co-leader to help share responsibilities. You won't get burned out and it is fun to share the experience. They can go on next year to lead your team or start a second one!

- Set a secondary goal for your team members. One example is: ask each team member to recruit at least one more person to walk with the team this year. If successful, you have doubled the size of your team.

- Offer fun incentives for the team members who raise the most money, recruit the most team members, and is the most enthusiastic: like a free ice cream sundae coupon, a car wash coupon, etc.

- Keep everyone aware of how the team is doing and any significant dates leading up to the day of the event via email.

- If you decide on a fundraising event, it should be held on pay day Friday, and advertised well in advance with colorful eye-catching flyers. Theme decorations and music helps set the mood.

- Have a Yard Sale which is a win-win because one person's trash truly is another person's treasure. Employees can get rid of their trash, and buy found treasure. Car wash, bake sales, department party, and picnics also work to get your team excited about Walk day and to get a jump on donations. This might attract new walk team members too.

- Hold a Spaghetti Supper at the lunch hour. $5/plate included spaghetti, garlic bread, drink and two fried Oreos. Use crock pot recipes for the spaghetti, so it isn't messy. Get Coke to donate the drinks (Don't be afraid to ask those

vendors you do business with for donations.
They might surprise you!)

- Invite contestants to enter their favorite recipe in
  a Chili Cook-Off. $5 gets you a taste of each
  entry, and a bowl of your favorite along with
  drink and dessert. All food should be donated.
  People can decorate their table, so you can have
  a separate award for that as well.

- Hold a Hot Dog Sale with a carnival theme with
  cotton candy and popcorn. Coke can donate the
  use of a trailer so you can set up outside. (Just
  ask, all they can say is no!)

- A Raffle can be very successful. Solicit
  donations and remember who your "audience" is.
  In one workplace raffle, over $100 was raised
  raffling a small tin of pull candy, because the
  employee's 90 year old mother is famous in the
  community for her skill with this candy.

- Consider a Pancake Breakfast: Wendy's,
  Applebee's and other local businesses will host
  pancake breakfasts and similar events. Ask
  around!

- Keep folks interested in the fundraising events
  by celebrating them. Take pictures then make a
  scrapbook or DVD. Have a potluck or other get
  together.

- Designate a day when all of your team members wear their Walk T-shirt - to work, to a family gathering, celebration picnic etc.

- Have a drawing for a day off from work. Ask the manager of your department to donate a paid day off to the winner of a drawing. Sell tickets for $5-$25 to your co-workers (this is an easy way for most companies/businesses to contribute without donating cash).

- Place collection jar with a personalized label on your desk and in common break areas for "impulse" donations.

- Hold a 50 / 50 opportunity drawing for a certain time period: a week, two weeks or a month. Half the money goes to the 2010AMIWalk and the other half goes to the winner of the drawing.

About the Author

Blair Young is a National Walk Manager for NAMI, the National Alliance on Mental Illness. He is responsible for assisting local affiliates and state organizations conduct successful NAMIWalks and works with Walks from New England across the Midwest and into the South. He is a native of Ohio and previously served as the Director of Development for NAMI Ohio.

Before joining NAMI in October 2000, Mr. Young spent 20 years in private business as owner-operator of a chain of restaurants near Columbus, Ohio. During that time, he served on numerous community boards and led fund raising campaigns for many area non-profits.

Mr. Young resides in southeastern Massachusetts with his wife, Maggie who is the director of a partial hospital program at a regional behavioral healthcare provider.